New Careers for the
21st Century:
Finding Your Role in
the Global Renewal

CAREERS IN GREEN ENERGY:

FUELING THE WORLD WITH RENEWABLE RESOURCES

New Careers for the 21st Century: Finding Your Role in the Global Renewal

CAREERS IN GREEN ENERGY:
FUELING THE WORLD WITH RENEWABLE RESOURCES

ENVIRONMENTAL SCIENCE & PROTECTION:
KEEPING OUR PLANET GREEN

FREELANCE AND TECHNICAL WRITERS:
WORDS FOR SALE

GREEN CONSTRUCTION:
CREATING ENERGY-EFFICIENT, LOW-IMPACT BUILDINGS

MEDIA IN THE 21ST CENTURY:
ARTISTS, ANIMATORS, AND GRAPHIC DESIGNERS

MEDICAL TECHNICIANS:
HEALTH-CARE SUPPORT FOR THE 21ST CENTURY

MODERN MECHANICS:
MAINTAINING TOMORROW'S GREEN VEHICLES

THE PHARMACEUTICAL INDUSTRY:
BETTER MEDICINE FOR THE 21ST CENTURY

PHYSICIANS' ASSISTANTS & NURSES:
NEW OPPORTUNITIES IN THE 21ST-CENTURY HEALTH SYSTEM

SOCIAL WORKERS: *FINDING SOLUTIONS FOR TOMORROW'S SOCIETY*

TOMORROW'S ENTERPRISING SCIENTISTS:
COMPUTER SOFTWARE DESIGNERS AND SPECIALISTS

TOMORROW'S TEACHERS:
URBAN LEADERSHIP, EMPOWERING STUDENTS & IMPROVING LIVES

TOMORROW'S TRANSPORTATION:
GREEN SOLUTIONS FOR AIR, LAND, & SEA

21ST-CENTURY COUNSELORS:
NEW APPROACHES TO MENTAL HEALTH & SUBSTANCE ABUSE

THERAPY JOBS IN EDUCATIONAL SETTINGS:
SPEECH, PHYSICAL, OCCUPATIONAL & AUDIOLOGY

New Careers for the
21st Century:
Finding Your Role in
the Global Renewal

CAREERS IN GREEN ENERGY:

FUELING THE WORLD WITH RENEWABLE RESOURCES

by Camden Flath

Mason Crest Publishers

CAREERS IN GREEN ENERGY:

FUELING THE WORLD WITH RENEWABLE RESOURCES

MASON CREST PUBLISHERS INC.
370 Reed Road
Broomall, Pennsylvania 19008
(866)MCP-BOOK (toll free)
www.masoncrest.com

First Printing
9 8 7 6 5 4 3 2 1

Library of Congress Cataloging-in-Publication Data

Flath, Camden, 1987–
   Careers in green energy : fueling the world with renewable resources / by Camden Flath.
       p. cm. — (New careers for the 21st century)
   Includes bibliographical references and index.
   ISBN 978-1-4222-1812-9   ISBN 978-1-4222-1811-2 (series)
   ISBN 978-1-4222-2033-7 (ppb)   ISBN 978-1-4222-2032-0 (series ppb)
   1. Clean energy industries—Vocational guidance—Juvenile literature. 2. Renewable energy sources—Vocational guidance—Juvenile literature. I. Title.
   HD9502.5.C542F55 2011
   333.79'4023—dc22
                          2010020683

Produced by Harding House Publishing Service, Inc.
www.hardinghousepages.com
Interior Design by MK Bassett-Harvey.
Cover design by Torque Advertising + Design.
Printed in USA by Bang Printing.

CONTENTS

INTRODUCTION...6

CHAPTER 1:
WHY IS GREEN ENERGY IMPORTANT?...9

CHAPTER 2:
TYPES OF GREEN ENERGY...21

CHAPTER 3:
CAREERS IN GREEN ENERGY...31

CHAPTER 4:
EDUCATION AND TRAINING...43

CHAPTER 5:
THE FUTURE OF GREEN ENERGY JOBS...51

FURTHER READING...58

FIND OUT MORE ON THE INTERNET...59

BIBLIOGRAPHY...60

INDEX...62

PICTURE CREDITS...63

ABOUT THE AUTHOR/ABOUT THE CONSULTANT...64

INTRODUCTION

Be careful as you begin to plan your career.

To get yourself in the best position to begin the career of your dreams, you need to know what the "green world" will look like and what jobs will be created and what jobs will become obsolete. Just think, according to the Bureau of Labor Statistics, the following jobs are expected to severely decline by 2012:

- word processors and data-entry keyers

- stock clerks and order fillers

- secretaries

- electrical and electronic equipment assemblers

- computer operators

- telephone operators

- postal service mail sorters and processing-machine operators

- travel agents

These are just a few of the positions that will decrease or become obsolete as we move forward into the century.

You need to know what the future jobs will be. How do you find them? One way is to look where money is being invested. Many firms and corporations are now making investments in startup and research enterprises. These companies may become the "Microsoft" and "Apple" of the twenty-first century. Look at what is being researched and what technology is needed to obtain the results.

Green world, green economy, green technology—they all say the same things: the way we do business today is changing. Every industry will be shaped by the world's new focus on creating a sustainable lifestyle, one that won't deplete our natural and economic resources.

The possibilities are unlimited. Almost any area that will conserve energy and reduce the dependency on fossil fuels is open to new and exciting career paths. Many of these positions have not even been identified yet and will only come to light as the technology progresses and new discoveries are made in the way we use that technology. And the best part about this is that our government is behind us. The U.S. government wants to help you get the education and training you'll need to succeed and grow in this new and changing economy. The U.S. Department of Labor has launched a series of initiatives to support and promote green job creation. To view the report, visit: www.dol.gov/dol/green/earthday_reportA.pdf.

The time to decide on your future is now. This series, NEW CAREERS FOR THE 21ST CENTURY: FINDING YOUR ROLE IN THE GLOBAL RENEWAL, can act as the first step toward your continued education, training, and career path decisions. Take the first steps that will lead you—and the planet—to a productive and sustainable future.

Mike Puglisi
Department of Labor, District I Director (New York/New Jersey)
IAWP (International Association of Workforce Professionals)

A [hu]man is related to all nature.

—Ralph Waldo Emerson

ABOUT THE QUOTE

During the nineteenth and twentieth centuries, many people lived in cities and worked in factories. They forgot that human beings depended on nature for their lives. Today, problems with pollution and climate change have reminded us all of how dependent we are on nature. Many twenty-first-century careers reflect this new awareness. Jobs in green energy offer you an opportunity to do your part to protect our planet.

CHAPTER 1
WHY IS GREEN ENERGY IMPORTANT?

Think of all the ways you use energy throughout your day. Every time you charge your cell phone, turn on a light, or fill up your car with gasoline, you are using energy. Even when you eat a meal, you are using some of the world's energy. Electricity—usually produced by burning coal—was needed not only for the lights you turn on but also to power the machines that made the parts of both your cell phone and your car. Gasoline—a product of oil drilled from deep underground or the ocean's floor—was used to fuel the trucks that delivered the food you eat to the supermarket. Gasoline was also consumed when the materials for your clothes were shipped to the factories where they were made—and then again when the clothes you wear went to the store where you bought them.

For many millions of people around the world, energy *consumption* has become an *indispensable* part of today's modern lifestyle—but the sources of energy we use are both damaging to the environment and limited in supply. Unlike energy sources that can be *depleted* over time and harm the environmental (such as oil and coal), however, *renewable*, green energy sources such as solar and wind power can provide electricity without damaging the air, water, and land.

YOUR ROLE IN THE ENERGY CRISIS

You've probably heard a lot about ways you can conserve energy and recycle products, and those are important ways to contribute the solution to the world's energy crisis. Today's youth will also become part of tomorrow's workforce, and finding a career that is not only satisfying and interesting, but also in line with the needs of a rapidly changing world, will allow you to make a difference in the world where you live. On top of that, of course, it can lead to a fulfilling, as well as successful career.

In a variety of industries, new and old, the demand for workers with an understanding of renewable resources is expected to rise rapidly in the next decade. Many occupations related to green energy are on track to grow faster than the average rate for all occupations. Young people who enter a green energy career will not only be working in an exciting new field, but they will also help to plan the world's energy future.

ENERGY AND CLIMATE CHANGE

In order to get energy from coal, oil, or natural gas, the three most-used energy sources in the United States, they must be burned. Burning these fossil fuels increases levels of greenhouse gases in the Earth's atmosphere. Greenhouse gases prevent heat from leaving our atmosphere and entering space—like the glass walls and roof of a greenhouse—leading over time to the rising of the overall temperature of our planet.

Crude oil is drawn up from underground wells using some type of pumping system. The pumpjacks pictured here mechanically lift about 1.3 to 10.6 gallons (5 to 40 liters) of oil with each stroke.

Greenhouse gases play an important role in keeping the surface of the Earth warm enough to support life. As the amounts of these gases in the atmosphere increases, however, the temperature of the Earth is rising beyond previous record highs. The National Oceanic and Atmospheric Administration (NOAA) and NASA report that, over the last one hundred years, the average surface temperature of the Earth has risen by between 1.2 and 1.4°F (.67 and .78°C). In addition, the eight warmest years recorded since 1850 have occurred in the last twelve years, and 2005 was the warmest year ever recorded. If levels of greenhouse gases continue to climb, it is estimated that the surface temperature of the Earth could increase between 3.2 and 7.2°F (1.78 and 4°C) above levels recorded in 1998 before the end of the twenty-first century. The rising temperature of the Earth's surface also leads to diminished snow and ice cover, altered rainfall levels, and melting sea ice that will increase sea levels, all of which have the potential to directly affect human lives.

Though scientists are sure that burning fossil fuels adds increased amounts of greenhouse gases to the atmosphere, leading to climate change, they are not sure exactly what changes the climate will experience as a result. What is clear, however, is that the burning of fossil fuels for energy has a negative impact on our atmosphere, our climate, and our planet as a whole.

GREENHOUSE GAS EMISSIONS

According to the United States Environmental Protection Agency, over 85 percent of the greenhouse gases produced worldwide come from the United States. America is an energy hog!

These greenhouse gas *emissions* are a result of burning fossil fuels for energy, as well as other industrial activities (carbon dioxide emissions unrelated to the burning of fossil fuels also accounts for some of the greenhouse gases emitted in the United States). Of all the energy-related greenhouse gas emissions in the United States, more than 50 percent come from large sources, including power plants. About one-third of all U.S emissions come from transportation. The rest of the emissions come from industry, agriculture, and waste management, as well as a few other sources.

THE ENERGY SOURCES WE USE TODAY

In the United States, coal, oil, and natural gas provide most of the power industries and individuals use. These forms of energy are called fossil fuels. The fossil fuels we use today are, in fact, decomposed plant and animal matter that has been exposed to millions of years of heat and pressure underground. Burning fossil fuels in vehicle engines and power plants produces energy. Since it took millions of years to create coal, oil, and natural gas, these energy sources are all nonrenewable, meaning they cannot be replenished naturally in an amount of time that allows for our current levels of consumption. In addition, using each of the three—coal, oil, and natural gas—causes long-term environmental harm.

COAL

In order to obtain energy from coal, humans must mine it from underground, transport it to power plants, and burn it. Inside power plants, coal is burned in a coal-fired boiler, creating steam. This steam turns a turbine, producing electricity and powering homes and businesses around the country. In 2003, the United States used more than 1.1 billion tons of coal, according to the Environmental Protection Agency.

ENVIRONMENTAL IMPACT OF COAL

As is the case with many modern energy sources, getting energy from coal has a variety of harmful effects on the environment.

When coal is burned in power plants, carbon dioxide, sulfur dioxide, and mercury are emitted, as well as other pollutants.

In addition to the atmospheric pollution that results from burning coal for energy, the process of extracting coal from the ground causes a great deal of environmental destruction.

Mining and transporting coal also produce greenhouse gases, including methane, a gas vented from mines because it can be a danger to workers.

The boilers used at power plants require water to produce steam. This water becomes polluted when it is used in the boiler or the boiler's cooling system. If this water is released into a lake, river, or other body of water, it can harm wildlife or humans who use those water resources. Mining runoff can also contaminate nearby rivers or lakes.

Coal-fired power plants damage the land they occupy, polluting the soil with a variety of byproducts from electricity generation. Mining also damages the land, particularly surface mining, including mountain-top removal mining, a process that involves the explosion of large areas of land in order to access coal inside mountains.

OIL

Oil is burned in power plants to create electricity, and it is also used in transportation. In order to produce electricity from oil, it must first be extracted from underground, processed at a refinery, transported to power plants, and then burned. When oil is first removed from underground, it is called crude oil. At refineries, crude oil is turned into a variety of products, including gasoline, propane, jet fuel, and others. Like coal-fired power plants, oil-fired power plants burn oil to create steam to turn an electricity-generating turbine. Some power plants burn oil to create power, and then use the exhaust from the engine to turn a turbine, creating more energy. This is called a combined cycle.

ENVIRONMENTAL IMPACT OF OIL

Burning oil to create electricity, as well as burning oil products to fuel vehicles and industrial equipment, creates greenhouse gases. Drilling for oil can also lead to greenhouse gas emissions from the heavy machinery needed for oil extraction. Oil-fired power plants use large amounts of water to produce steam and in cooling systems. These power plants sometimes take water

Did You Know?

As of 2008, the Central Intelligence Agency, which collects various data on countries across the world, estimated that the United States consumed 19,500,000 barrels of oil each day, putting the yearly total at just over 7.1 billion barrels.

An oil spill can be an environmental disaster. This image shows a spill spreading out into the Gulf of Mexico in April of 2010.

from local resources, harming *aquatic ecosystems*. They also sometimes release polluted water into these same water sources. Oil spills during the transportation or extraction of oil can also seriously damage the aquatic environments and, in some cases, coastal businesses. Drilling can cause waterways to become contaminated with runoff, harming wildlife. The process of refining crude oil and burning oil at power plants can create solid waste that is toxic, as well.

NATURAL GAS

Like coal and oil, natural gas is burned in power plants to create electricity. Producing electricity using natural gas begins with extracting that gas from the earth by drilling. Gas is processed and refined at gas plants after extraction. Natural gas is transported to power plants by gas pipelines.

Power plants burn natural gas in a variety of ways to produce electricity. Some burn gas in a gas-fired boiler in order to create steam used to turn a turbine and generate power. More often, however, power plants burn natural gas in what is called a combustion turbine, a machine similar to an engine, which generates electricity. Some natural gas power plants are using the same combined cycle method that is being used to burn oil for electricity.

ENVIRONMENTAL IMPACT OF NATURAL GAS

Though not as environmentally damaging as the emissions from burning oil and coal for electricity, burning natural gas for power does create greenhouse gases. Specifically, methane leaks can occur during the transportation and burning of natural gas.

What Kind of Person Are You?

Career-counseling experts know that certain kinds of people do best in certain kinds of jobs. John L. Holland developed the following list of personality types and the kinds of jobs that are the best match for each type. See which one (or two) are most like you. The more you understand yourself, the better you'll be able to make a good career plan for yourself.

- **Realistic personality**: This kind of person likes to do practical, hands-on work. He or she will most enjoy working with materials that can be touched and manipulated, such as wood, steel, tools, and machinery. This personality type enjoys jobs that require working outdoors, but he or she does NOT enjoy jobs that require a lot of paperwork or close teamwork with others.

- **Investigative personality**: This personality type likes to work with ideas. He or she will enjoy jobs that require lots of thinking and researching. Jobs that require mental problem solving will be a good fit for this personality.

- **Artistic personality**: This type of person enjoys working with forms, designs, and patterns. She or he likes jobs that require self-expression—and that don't require following a definite set of rules.

- **Social personality**: Jobs that require lots of teamwork with others, as well as teaching others, are a good match for this personality type. These jobs often involve helping others in some way.

- **Enterprising personality**: This person will enjoy planning and starting new projects, even if that involves a degree of risk-taking. He or she is good at making decisions and leading others.

- **Conventional personality**: An individual with this type of personality likes to follow a clear set of procedures or routines. He or she doesn't want to be the boss but prefers to work under someone else's leadership. Jobs that require working with details and facts (more than ideas) are a good fit for this personality.

Did You Know?

According to the CIA World Factbook, the United States uses more oil per day than every country in the European Union and Japan combined. The United States ranks number one in oil use per day. The EU countries taken together rank second, while Japan ranks fourth, below Russia.

United States	19,500,000 barrels/ per day
European Union	14,390,000 barrels/ per day
Japan	4,785,000 barrels/ per day

Emissions of other greenhouse gases can be generated during extraction and treatment of natural gas. Though greenhouse gases are released in order to produce energy from natural gas, when compared to the emissions generated by coal-fired plants, natural gas power plants produce around half as much carbon dioxide.

Natural gas power plants require water for cooling systems, and they sometimes take that water from nearby waterways, damaging natural ecosystems, though less water is used in burning natural gas than coal or oil.

A life's work is born out of your visions, values, and ideals. It's giving life to your values, anchoring them in the everyday world of action.

—Laurence G. Boldt

ABOUT THE QUOTE

We need money to buy the things we need and want, but your career should be far more than a way to simply earn money. The work you do will help shape the world around you—and you'll find that the work you find most satisfying and exciting will be work that matches up with the things you care about most. Your career should be a way you use your interests and skills to make the world a better place.

CHAPTER **2**
TYPES OF GREEN ENERGY

R enewable energy comes from sources that cannot be depleted with overuse, or from sources that will replenish over an amount of time that will make using them *sustainable*. These resources cannot be used faster than they will be replenished naturally. While using oil, coal, and natural gas to power our civilization pollutes the air, water, and land, renewable energy sources like solar or wind power have little to no impact on the environment. For instance, because no fuels are burned in creating energy from wind, water, or sunlight, using these energy sources generates no greenhouse gases. Renewable, sustainable energy sources include:

• solar

• geothermal

• biomass

• landfill gas

• wind

• hydroelectricity

Though renewable energy accounts for only a small amount of the overall energy used in the United States, and it will take many years before wind or solar energy is used as widely as fossil fuels, use of these energy sources is on the rise. As each becomes more widely used, workers will be needed in emerging industries, helping to create the technology and infrastructure needed to use renewable resources to power the modern world.

SOLAR

Solar power systems use sunlight to create electricity. Electricity can be produced using sunlight in two ways: photovoltaic and solar thermal technology. Photovoltaic systems are made up of panels of conductive materials. A chemical reaction caused by sunlight hitting the conductive materials produces electricity. Solar thermal systems use mirrors to focus the sun's energy on liquid, often water, in order to create steam that will turn a turbine, creating electricity.

ENVIRONMENTAL IMPACTS

Converting sunlight to energy has no impact on air quality because it does not involve burning fuel. Photovoltaic solar power systems do not need to use any water, and while solar thermal systems use water to create steam in some cases, the water can be re-used safely afterward.

The production of solar photovoltaic panels can create residue that may be harmful to the environment and must be specially handled. This

These panels are part of the largest photovoltaic solar power plant in the United States at Nellis Air Force Base. Completed in December 2007, the solar arrays produce 15 megawatts of power.

material is only created in very small amounts, however. In addition, solar thermal technology requires more land than photo-voltaic panels (which are usually placed on roofs). Installation does not damage the land itself, but land used for solar thermal systems cannot be used for other purposes, and may displace wildlife populations in some cases.

GEOTHERMAL

Geothermal energy is the heat energy created inside the Earth due to the high temperature of the Earth's core. Geothermal energy creates hot water and steam that can be used to turn turbines and create electricity. We can also get power from geothermal sources by pumping water underground, then bringing it back to the surface newly heated and ready to create electricity.

ENVIRONMENTAL IMPACTS

No fuels are burned when using geothermal energy, so the emissions from getting electricity with this method are nonexistent. In addition, no solid waste is produced when using geothermal power.

Most of the water used in geothermal energy production can be released into the environment without any pollution at all. Some water, however, will be lost to evaporation during heating processes (both natural and partially assisted by technology). There is a possibility of polluting underground water resources during the extraction of water from the Earth, but the impact of drilling can be mitigated with proper practices.

BIOMASS

Biomass refers to the fuel created from organic material such as plant material. Biomass includes agricultural waste (corn husks, for instance), and it can also be used to create biofuel. Because crops can be replaced on a human time scale, biofuels are considered a renewable resource. In addition, using wastes for fuel is seen as sustainable, in that those materials would be disposed of if not recycled for fuel use. Biomass fuel can be burned at power plants for electricity, but it can also be used to power vehicles.

ENVIRONMENTAL IMPACTS

Burning biomass for fuel and electricity can cause some of the same emissions that burning fossil fuels can cause, but in lesser amounts, making their use more environmentally friendly. Using

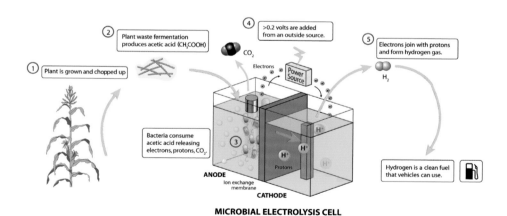

Fuel cells run by hydrogen are another energy technology being researched for the future. Researchers have designed a microbial electrolysis cell in which bacteria break up acetic acid (a product of plant waste fermentation) to produce hydrogen gas with a very small electric input from an outside source.

biomass fuels also produces some of the same pollution to waterways that fossil fuels do, but again in lesser amounts; there is also the possibility of contamination of water due to use of pesticides in the growth of crops used for biomass. Biomass crops also require a lot of land, possibly leading to environmental degradation of the soil.

LANDfILL GAS

By using small microorganisms to consume the waste that occupies landfills around the country and creating gas in the process, humans can use landfills to produce energy. As microorganisms decompose waste in landfills, they produce methane and carbon dioxide, both of which can be harnessed to create electrical power. Collecting and burning landfill gas can lead to recycled power depending on how much waste is located in a landfill. Around 365 landfills in the United States are creating power by burning landfill gas, according to the Environmental Protection Agency.

ENVIRONMENTAL IMPACTS

Burning landfill gas does create some harmful air emissions, but the amount of these emissions can change depending on the landfill. Using landfill gas to obtain energy keeps methane from entering the atmosphere by burning it off, and the carbon dioxide produced in the process is considered to be a natural part of the Earth's *carbon cycle*.

Getting energy from landfill gas requires little to no water, and it does not produce any solid waste. In addition, landfill gas doesn't require much, if any, land beyond what is already used by the landfill.

WIND

Wind turbines can be used to harness the movement of the wind to generate electricity. These turbines use two or three blades moved by the wind to turn a gear that produces electricity. A collection of many wind turbines together, used to power greater population centers, is called a wind farm. According to the EPA, the Rocky Mountain and Great Plains states have enough wind resources to provide enough electricity to meet anywhere between 10 to 25 percent of the power demands of those states.

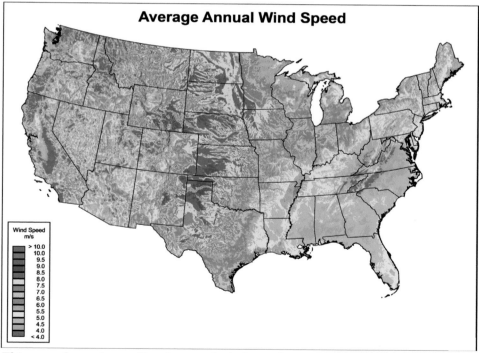

Average Annual Wind Speed

Wind Speed
m/s

> 10.0
10.0
9.5
9.0
8.5
8.0
7.5
7.0
6.5
6.0
5.5
5.0
4.5
4.0
< 4.0

This map shows the predicted annual wind speeds across the United States. Areas with annual average wind speeds around 6.5 m/s and greater at 80-m height are generally considered to have suitable wind resource for wind development.

ENVIRONMENTAL IMPACTS

There are no emissions generated by using wind turbines to create electricity, because no fuels are burned during any part of the process. In addition, this method of getting energy does not impact water resources in any significant ways and does not produce any solid waste.

Wind turbines and wind farms usually require land, but plans for offshore wind farms are also in progress. There has been some arguments about offshore wind farms defacing shoreline views, but the energy benefits of using large, offshore wind farms may outweigh *aesthetic* concerns.

Did You Know?
According to the EPA, the United States' hydroelectric power plants can supply energy equivalent to around 500 million barrels of oil.

Wind turbines can cause noise, which can disturb nearby residents. Turbines can also harm or kill birds, though newer technologies help alleviate the bulk of this problem.

HYDROELECTRICITY

Hydroelectric power creates electricity by harnessing the movement of water. In order to use the movement of water for power, humans must place dams in rivers. These dams then direct water through a turbine, creating electricity. After water passes through a hydroelectric power plant's turbine (connected to a generator), it is most often returned to the river or reservoir downstream from the dam.

ENVIRONMENTAL IMPACTS

Hydroelectric methods of power generation do not create any significant damage to air quality, contaminate water resources, or produce any solid waste. The drawbacks of using hydroelectric power include the potential damage to ecosystems where rivers are dammed for power plants. Hydroelectric power plants require a lot of land, which can lead to environmental *degradation* or animal habitat destruction. Dams can also alter the flow of rivers, affecting the natural environment and harming wildlife. Fish populations are most dramatically affected by hydroelectric power plants.

And all these new technologies, for all green energy sources, will require a host of workers to keep them running.

If You Have an Investigative Personality . . .

You may be happy in many green energy jobs where you will have opportunities to understand and solve problems. Your skills in math and science, as well as your curiosity, will make you a particularly good match for research-and-development jobs.

If You Have an Artistic Personality . . .

Green energy jobs may not be the best career choice for you, since careers in this field might not give you enough opportunities for creativity and self-expression. The future will need people who can think outside the box, though, people with creative ideas that will generate new ways to produce green energy, so don't automatically assume you can't find a place where you'd be happy in this career field.

Questions are the creative acts of intelligence.

—Frank Kingdon-Ward

ABOUT THE QUOTE

A good way to choose a career direction might be to think about the things that make you feel curious. What would you like to learn more about? What makes you feel curious and full of wonder? This feeling may be an arrow pointing you toward a life's career.

CHAPTER 3

CAREERS IN GREEN ENERGY

WORDS TO KNOW

infrastructure: The basic, underlying organization and framework of a system.

market data: Information about the current and past selling prices of stocks.

initiatives: Introductory steps.

The number of careers in green energy and related fields may be small today, but green energy is on track to be one of the largest sources of new jobs over the next several years, and on into the future. As the United States and the world move to increased use of renewable energy sources, more workers will be needed to create the technologies and *infrastructure* to provide energy in an environmentally friendly and sustainable way. New industries will emerge and old ones will change. Students in the classroom today may be leading new green energy industries in years to come.

RESEARCH-AND-DEVELOPMENT CAREERS

Much of the technology that will be needed to use green energy sources in the future is in development today. In the same way, the solar panels, biofuels, and other renewable energy sources that are being used today are the products of the research and development of the past. Research-and-development workers are vitally important to green energy industries, and they may help to create future, as-yet-unknown technologies that will shape how we use energy, leading to further innovation.

Research and development (often called R&D) consists of three kinds of work:

• basic research

• applied research

• development

Basic research is often theoretical and done without any specific goal in mind. Usually funded by government, universities, or nonprofit organizations, basic research is carried out to advance the understanding of scientists. Applied research connects basic research and business interests or consumer needs. This research is done with the goal of solving a particular problem with the results of basic research, but it may not yield any one perfected solution. Development is the refinement of research into a product that can be used by businesses, individuals, or the government. The majority of development is carried out by private industry with the intent to manufacture a final product. Almost all technological innovations in the last one hundred years have been the result of this process. In the same way, the green energy technologies of the future will be created and developed by workers in research and development.

Chemical and materials science research and development is one specialized field within the larger R&D field. Workers in chemical and materials science R&D work to create new molecules or materials that can be used in industry or by individuals. This includes searching for alternatives to oil, or changing the processes used by refineries in order to cut down on pollution and energy use. In addition, chemical and materials science R&D includes the development of fuel cells for use in vehicles. These fuel cells could dramatically decrease the need for gasoline.

Deborah Myers, a scientist from the Argonne National Laboratory, is involved in research and development of technology for use in new types of fuel cells.

ENGINEERING CAREERS

Engineers use their understanding of science and mathematics to create technical solutions to human problems. They work to translate the latest scientific discoveries into usable, everyday applications in order to meet the needs of a community or group of consumers. In many cases, these workers are involved in both the research-and-development and the manufacturing sides of emerging technology industries, including green energy.

Engineers may be responsible for the development of new products, systems, or technologies. During the design of a new project, engineers must understand the need they are trying to meet, finalize the concept by incorporating proven methods and research, and assess the feasibility of the project from both a cost and functionality perspective. These workers may also oversee the production or testing of the product created from their design.

ENGINEERING SPECIALTIES

Most engineers work in a specialized field of engineering. Within these engineering specialties, engineers may further specialize. Engineers may work in a single industry (such as energy) or on a single technology (such as power-producing wind turbines). What follows here are a few examples of engineering careers that will be important to the future of green energy.

ELECTRICAL ENGINEERS

Electrical engineers design and develop electrical equipment. They may also test the equipment or oversee its production. Electrical engineers usually specialize in power generation and transmission technology, such as the green energy systems that may be installed in a home or business. An electrical engineer may oversee the implementation of a solar power system, for instance.

ENVIRONMENTAL ENGINEERS

Environmental engineers use their knowledge of biology and chemistry to solve problems related to the environment. They work in pollution control, waste management, and public health. These workers may aide in a waste cleanup operation, advising officials on what to do. In some cases, environmental engineers may speak with regulators about how best to prevent further issues. These workers may be involved in a particular environmental issue, such as curbing greenhouse gas emissions or developing sustainable energy systems. Environmental engineers may also work as consultants, advising organizations and businesses about the best approach to a particular environmental problem.

MECHANICAL ENGINEERS

Mechanical engineering is a broad category, covering 238,000 workers (as of 2008). Mechanical engineers design and develop mechanical devices. These workers help create engines, industrial equipment, power-generation machinery, and other mechanical equipment. Mechanical engineers may supervise the production of machinery used in a wind turbine or hydroelectric dam. In the future, mechanical engineers will be increasingly needed to design and produce better green energy technology.

ENERGY ENGINEERS

Energy engineers design and carry out projects that improve energy efficiency and reduce energy costs. They may work on the construction of a building to make sure that it uses energy in the best possible way. These workers also create technical documentation for energy-efficiency projects, and report progress to their superiors. Energy engineers must be able to closely watch the energy use trends of an organization and recommend ways to improve efficiency or reduce cost.

SOLAR ENERGY SYSTEMS ENGINEER

Solar energy systems engineers design and implement solar power generation systems. They may speak with customers to evalu-

Scientists and engineers are important to the development of green energy technology, but in the end, the people who will bring it to consumers are the manufacturers and installation workers.

ate their solar power needs. Then, they design a system around that customer's home or business. They may also be responsible for maintaining a system after it is set up. Solar energy systems engineers often supervise installers and other workers during a solar power project.

WIND ENERGY ENGINEERS

Wind energy engineers design wind farm systems and prepare the sites on which they are built. They help design the components of wind turbines, often preparing technical documentation. These workers oversee the implementation of wind farm systems sometimes including the manufacturing of windmill parts.

Did You Know?
In 2008, 1.6 million engineers had work in their field, according to the Bureau of Labor Statistics. Of these 1.6 million, 54,300 were environmental engineers.

Wind energy engineers also monitor the performance of wind farms, and the parts that make up wind turbines, coordinating repairs in some cases.

MANUFACTURING JOBS

Once scientists and engineers have created a new technology, it must then be made real by workers in the manufacturing industry. Even though, taken as a whole, manufacturing employment is projected to decline in the United States in the near future, green energy manufacturing jobs will need to be filled as renewable sources of energy like solar and wind power become an increasingly important part of America's energy economy.

Manufacturing jobs related to green energy are mostly in the sub-category of machinery manufacturing jobs. These workers will be needed to create the turbines needed for wind farms and hydroelectric dams, as well as other equipment needed to extract energy from renewable sources. In addition, aerospace and motor vehicle parts manufacturing will increasingly need workers who can build engines that can take advantage of greener power, such as biomass, electric, and fuel cell technology.

Manufacturers may work with engineers to understand the design of a product or technology. Once the design is completed, the product, machine, or technology goes into production. More than half of all manufacturing jobs are in production. For example, metal workers create the parts needed in a certain piece of equipment or technology. These workers might maintain or even program complicated computerized manufacturing equipment in order to complete a project. Industrial production managers oversee the creation of all the parts of the final product, making sure each worker involved in production completes their task competently. Assemblers and fabricators take finished parts created by other workers and put together the final product, be it a solar panel or windmill blade.

OTHER CAREERS RELATED TO GREEN ENERGY

While scientists, engineers, and manufacturers all have a hand in developing the technology that allows humans to use renewable energy sources, many other workers will be need in related fields. This includes workers need to install energy systems, examine *market data* for green energy providers, advise companies as they turn to using green energy, and many others. Provided here are a few examples of other careers in green energy.

WIND ENERGY PROJECT MANAGER

Wind energy project managers are responsible for the development of wind energy business. They may lead studies, seek permits, or make proposals in order to further wind energy projects. These workers may also supervise the construction of wind energy projects, keeping the budget of the project in mind. Wind energy project managers may also give advice on the design of new projects, as well as where they will be built.

SOLAR ENERGY INSTALLATION MANAGERS

Solar energy installation managers oversee crews of workers who install solar photovoltaic (PV) systems or thermal energy systems in businesses and homes. These workers may need to visit sites to speak with customers and evaluate their solar power system needs. They plan the installation of photovoltaic solar power systems or solar thermal systems and coordinate their installation with solar technicians and installers. Some solar energy installation managers are also responsible for providing technical assistance to the workers they supervise on installation jobs. They may also test a solar power system once it is installed. In addition, they may need to educate customers on how to maintain their system, answering any questions their clients may have.

ENERGY BROKERS

Energy brokers buy and sell energy for clients and businesses. They speak with buyers and sellers of energy and negotiate the purchase or sale between parties. These workers may need to explain a particular deal or transaction with customers, as well as answer questions on energy markets and alternative sources of energy. Energy brokers must observe energy markets so that they understand the price of energy and are able to advise their clients accordingly.

SUSTAINABILITY SPECIALISTS

Sustainability specialists are experts in understanding the long-term impact of energy use, waste generation, recycling, and natural resource use. Companies and organizations hire these workers to plan sustainable ways of building, providing energy, and managing waste. They create sustainability goals and strategies to reach those milestones. Sustainability specialists may present to a company's executives, for example, their plan to make a company greener. They then provide reports on the progress of the plans and promote their *initiatives* to the public if it is required. These workers will be essential in providing advice to companies about how they can use alternative, green energy in powering their business.

ENVIRONMENTAL ECONOMISTS

Environmental economists examine and explain the financial benefits of using environmentally friendly methods of building, powering, and running businesses and homes. This work includes researching the relationship between the environment and the economy, recommending polices that will result in financial and environmental sustainability, assessing the costs of certain ways of doing business, and many other responsibilities. Though not directly involved in the production of power from green energy sources, governmental and private organizations will employ these workers in order to make the best use of current and future green energy systems.

GEOTHERMAL PRODUCTION MANAGERS

Geothermal production managers work at geothermal power plants. They maintain and oversee the equipment of the power plant, in addition to making sure the plant operates safely. Their work also includes supervising plant employees, managing budgets, inspecting the operation of specific geothermal plant processes or procedures, as well as many other tasks. Geothermal production managers will be in higher demand as geothermal power plants become more prevalent around the globe.

These are just a few of the many, many jobs that the need for green energy will create in the years to come!

If You Have a Social Personality . . .

You may enjoy working in a green-energy job where you will have direct contact with customers. These jobs will give you opportunities to help people who need you. Your helpful, friendly nature will be an asset for you, and you can know that your job makes an important contribution to the well-being of the entire world.

Technology is destructive only in the hands of people who do not realize that they are one and the same process as the universe.

—Alan Watts

ABOUT THE QUOTE

Technology has gotten a bad name. We talk about "getting back to nature," as though if we could all do so we would solve all the Earth's problems. But the reality is that we need technology to solve the problems we have created (such as climate change and pollution). If you choose a career in green energy, you will be using technology in harmony with nature.

CHAPTER 4
EDUCATION AND TRAINING

WORDS TO KNOW

bachelor's degree: The degree awarded to a person who has completed an undergraduate course of study, usually taking four years.

master's degree: The degree awarded to a person who has completed a specialized course of graduate study, usually taking one to two years.

Ph.D.: Also called a doctorate; the highest academic degree a person can earn, usually taking three years of course work and the acceptance of a written dissertation.

apprenticeships: Training periods during which students study under more experienced workers in order to learn a trade.

secondary education: The stage of education after elementary school and lasting through graduation from high school.

post-secondary education: Education after graduation from high school, including undergraduate and graduate studies.

Workers in green energy and related careers have a wide range of educational backgrounds. Many careers require a *bachelor's degree*, while others may need an advanced degree, or only a high school diploma and work experience.

Research and Development

Education and Training

The overwhelming majority of jobs in scientific research and development are open only to workers who hold degrees in science and engineering fields. More workers in R&D have bachelor's degrees or higher than in all other industries. Senior researchers will need to hold advanced degrees such as *master's degrees* or *Ph.D.* degrees, though there are also high-level starting positions that will require workers to have advanced degrees as well.

Advancement

As scientists and engineers gain experience in their field of research and development, they may advance to become senior researchers or managers of R&D projects. Higher-level work assignments and promotions are usually given out based on level of expertise in a specific subject or technology. Taking on larger projects or coordinating more than one kind of work at once are ways for workers in R&D to prove their skills.

Engineering

Education and Training

Most engineers entering the workforce hold bachelor's degrees in one of the many engineering specialties. Some jobs in research may require that workers hold an advanced engineering degree. Engineers also need to continue to educate themselves, since technology changes and advances. Certification is a good way for engineers who are already in the workforce to expand their skills and further their education, making them more competitive in the job market.

ADVANCEMENT

Engineers who are just starting their careers may work under more experienced engineers in order to gain on-the-job work experience. After gaining experience in their specialization, engineers may advance to become supervisors or technical specialists in their chosen field. Some may go on to sales departments of companies where they can advise sales representatives about the technical aspects of a product or service.

MANUFACTURING

EDUCATION AND TRAINING

Most manufacturing jobs today require that workers have at least a high school diploma. In order to qualify for production jobs that require manufacturers to do skilled work with machines (as is the case with many of the green energy jobs of today and tomorrow), many workers will need to have bachelor's degrees or complete coursework at community colleges. Some workers may go into *apprenticeships* in order to learn the skills they will need.

Management jobs in manufacturing usually require a bachelor's degree, though experience in production may allow workers to advance to these positions. Workers in green manufacturing management may have degrees in mechanical or electrical engineering.

ADVANCEMENT

Experienced manufacturing workers may be promoted to supervisory jobs. Advancement in manufacturing careers depends largely on work experience, though green energy manufacturing jobs in the future will likely require solid computer skills and understanding of complicated technology.

EDUCATION AND EXPERIENCE FOR OTHER GREEN ENERGY CAREERS

Workers in other jobs related to green energy have different backgrounds from the scientists, engineers, and manufacturers creating green energy technology. Those involved with the economic issues of green energy, for instance, may have a degree (bachelor's, master's, or beyond) in economics. Workers in the field of sustainability may take courses in environmental studies offered in a bachelor's program available at many four-year colleges, focusing on classes in green energy sources. Increasingly, students who wish to go into green careers, including those in energy, can tailor the college courses they take to their interests, as many more colleges and universities are offering environmental studies and sustainability courses at both the undergraduate and graduate levels.

In addition to careers that require a *secondary* or *postsecondary education*, many people hiring green energy workers in a variety of fields will be satisfied with applicants who have a high school diploma and work experience that proves they can do the job. Many solar installers or installation managers have a background in construction, for instance, while expert roofers may find work installing solar panels onto the roofs of homes or businesses. With time, these workers (who may have no formal education in solar power) can gain enough work experience to have steady work, or even a full-time career in the emerging solar industry.

Some workers will be able to make a living as consultants, advising individuals and businesses on green energy and sustainability choices. These workers may be able to enter these careers thanks to solid, specialized education or by having extensive work experience in a particular field.

Others may find careers in education, teaching students about the benefits of using renewable energy sources. These workers may not be involved directly in production of green energy, but they will influence how we use energy in the future by educating tomorrow's workers, business owners, and industry leaders.

If You Have a Realistic Personality . . .

You will be able to find many jobs in green energy that will be a good choice for you. Since you'll probably want a job setting where you work with tools and machines, allowing you to express the practical and mechanical side of your nature, manufacturing or installation jobs may be the best match for your skills and preferences.

Real-Life Career
Rebekah Hren, Solar Photovoltaic (PV) Installer

Rebekah Hren loves her job because she gets to promote solar power, but she also says she enjoys the thrill of working in a new industry. "It's kind of like the Wild West," she says. "It's a fun industry to be in right now." Rebekah works as a solar photovoltaic (PV) installer. She sets up solar energy systems, including solar panels and the electrical wiring that transports power throughout a home or business.

Solar photovoltaic systems, also known as solar cells, convert sunlight into electricity. Most of the jobs Rebekah does consist of placing solar panels on the roofs of buildings or houses. Solar cells are also produced as roof tiles and siding. Over the course of a few days (for home installation), Rebekah must install the solar cells, wire them to an inverter (which converts the direct current of the solar cells to usable energy), and test the system to make sure it works correctly. Some local governments require that workers have an electrician's license to become a PV installer, so that they understand how to wire the solar cells to the inverter. Rebekah has a license and does all the wiring on her jobs. Larger jobs installing solar power systems in office buildings or businesses may be completed over the course of months, with a work environment similar to construction jobs where work is done on site.

Rebekah also warns that people looking for work in solar installation need to know the potential risks, as well as the benefits, including the heights at which solar installers must work. "The scariest part of the work is being up on the roof," she says. "You have to be a certain type of person to climb up on roofs and do high-voltage electrical wiring."

Rebekah says she gets the most enjoyment from her job when considering her positive impact on the future of energy use. "What I really love is installing a system and knowing that it will be creating clean energy for twenty-five years," she says. "It's exciting to be making a difference."

You must be the change you wish to see in the world.

—Mahatma Gandhi

CHAPTER 5
THE FUTURE OF GREEN ENERGY JOBS

WORDS TO KNOW

subsidies: Grants of money, usually given by the government to encourage commercial growth in certain fields.

incentives: Rewards or benefits offered to encourage certain actions.

According to the Bureau of Labor Statistics, electricity produced from renewable sources, such as solar or wind power, is one of the fastest growing parts of the electric power industry. As a whole, renewable energy sources are becoming an increasingly larger part of energy production in the United States. The Energy Information Administration reported in 2006 that renewable energy sources accounted for around 7 percent of the electrical power in the United States. This percentage is growing even larger as renewable forms of energy become more widely used. In 2007, for instance, electric power generation from non-hydroelectric renewable energy sources grew 7 percent over the year before.

Subsidies, tax cuts, and grants given by the government (at the federal, state, and local levels) make the move to green energy more economically desirable. This will also lead to increased hiring in renewable energy-related occupations and grow the industry as a whole.

Each state's level of renewable energy usage is different. If a state government or local governments within that state invest more in green energy, they are more likely to see industry and utility companies shift to using more renewable energy sources. The Texas state government has made investment in wind energy a priority, for example, and as of fall 2009, the state had more wind energy production than any other state in the United States. Geography is also somewhat important in determining where jobs and industry growth in green energy sectors are most likely to be found. (For instance, regions that have more cloudy days will not invest in solar energy as much as sunny regions.)

Did You Know?
According to information from the American Solar Energy Society, around 106,000 workers had jobs in green energy industries in 2006.

The growth in green energy use will also help drive employment in new industries that spring up around green energy, or in old industries hoping to shift their focus to renewable, environmentally friendly ways of providing energy. For workers looking to make a difference in the future of energy use, help the environment, prevent widespread emissions of greenhouse gases that contribute to climate change, and find successful, fulfilling careers, the increasing use of green energy is good news.

In addition to new workers entering careers in green energy, many workers who currently work in the energy-production industries may be able to transfer their skills to new green industries. In a report by the U.S. Bureau of Labor Statistics, Ann Randazzo, the director of the Center for Energy Workforce Development, says that "jobs in renewable energy are not all that different from jobs in traditional energy sources." Randazzo says that someone who has been trained in the skills needed to work on the electrical grid system, for

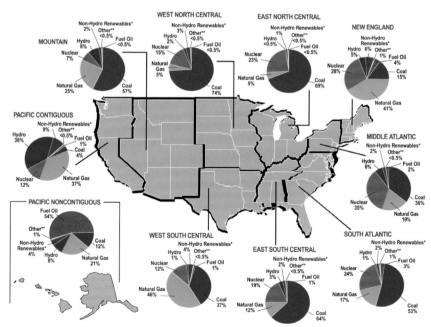

This map from 2009, shows that across the United States, a diverse mix of fuel is used to generate electricity. The percentage of green energy sources is increasing each year.

instance, will likely have little trouble learning the skills needed to work on wind-power systems, including wind farm turbines.

THE FUTURE OF WIND AND SOLAR ENERGY

Wind and solar energy are two of the fastest growing sources of both renewable energy and green energy jobs. The technology that exists today is sufficient for the United States to get more than enough energy to power the entire country, but it has yet to be implemented on a wide enough scale to make that possible. Workers entering green energy careers in wind and solar power today are helping to shape the future of American and global energy use.

> **Did You Know?**
> According to a study by the Renewable and Appropriate Energy Laboratory located at the University of California at Berkeley (cited by the Bureau of Labor Statistics in a 2008 document on energy jobs in the United States), renewable energy creates more jobs per kilowatt hour than fossil fuel-based energy.

WIND

Wind-based power generation is the single fastest growing energy source in the United States, according to a 2008 report by the Bureau of Labor Statistics on energy production jobs. In 2007, for instance, wind energy generation increased by 21 percent. The United States Environmental Protection Agency predicts that wind power could account for as much as 20 percent of the electrical energy needed in the United States by the year 2030.

Tracking the exact number of jobs in wind power currently is difficult, as the Department of Labor's Bureau of Labor Statistics does not keep track of the number of workers employed in wind power. The American Solar Energy Society, a group advocating the use of solar energy and other renewable energy sources, however, estimates that about 16,000 workers were involved in the construction, installation, and maintenance of wind turbines in 2006. This number does not include the number of workers involved in wind power indirectly. Wind farms are up and running in thirty-four states across the country, where they were once concentrated in only a few states, allowing for increased hiring in wind power throughout the United States.

President Barack Obama is pushing for wind power to take a central role in America's energy future, as well. Government investment in wind power projects, as well as *incentives* to companies that use green energy sources like wind power, will drive further employment growth in industries directly and indirectly related to the field.

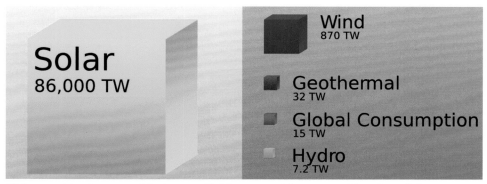

This graphic shows worldwide available renewable energy. The size of the cubes represents the amount of available geothermal, hydropower, wind and solar energy in terawatts (TW).

SOLAR

Though the technology that allows us to produce electricity from sunlight has existed for some time, recent investment by government at all levels has led to more solar power technology being used by homes and businesses. By increasing the number of incentives (such as tax breaks) to homeowners who turn to solar power, the government can help drive the demand for solar power technology. This will in turn increase demand for workers in the industries related to green power.

The American Solar Energy Society estimates that around 7,600 people worked in the solar photovoltaic and solar thermal industries in 2006. Though this number is relatively small com-

One of Barack Obama's aims is to make the country greener. His administration's green energy initiative has six major goals, one of which is to ensure 10 percent of our electricity comes from renewable sources by 2012, and 25 percent by 2025.

If You Have an Enterprising Personality . . .

Like most fields, green energy jobs have higher-level managerial positions that will allow you opportunities to use your leadership skills and express your ambitions. Be aware, though, that most jobs have few entry-level positions that are managerial, so you need to be prepared to put in your time at lower levels of responsibility, proving over time both your skills and your ability to make decisions and lead others. Who knows? One day, you might even own your own green energy business!

If You Have a Conventional Personality . . .

You'll be able to find jobs within the green energy field that will be a good match for you. As a manufacturing worker, you would have plenty of opportunities to work with machines in a set, orderly way. Since you're good at working with written records and numbers in a systematic way, you might also do well as an inspector in this field.

pared to some other occupations, keep in mind that renewable energy industries are new and only just now beginning to expand rapidly. Most of the workers in the solar power industry are solar installers, who work to put up solar panels and connect them to the electrical systems of homes and businesses. About 5,000 people currently work in this occupation, though the number is expected to grow alongside the solar power industry.

"We know the country that harnesses the power of clean, renewable energy will lead the twenty-first century," said President Barack Obama in his address to Congress on February 24, 2009. If you find a career in green energy, you too will be one of the future's leaders!

FURTHER READING

Brezina, Corona. *Jobs in Sustainable Energy.* New York: Rosen Publishing Group, 2010.

DeGalan, Julie. *Great Jobs for Environmental Studies Majors.* New York: McGraw-Hill, 2008.

Fehl, Pamela. *Energy (Green Careers).* New York: Ferguson, 2010.

Greenland, Paul R. and Annamarie L. Sheldon. *Career Opportunities in Conservation and the Environment.* New York: Checkmark Books, 2007.

McNamee, Gregory. *Careers in Renewable Energy.* Masonville, Colo.: PixyJack Press, 2008.

FIND OUT MORE ON THE INTERNET

American Academy of Environmental Engineers
www.aaee.net

American Solar Energy Society
www.ases.org

American Wind Energy Association
www.awea.org

Department of Energy, Energy Efficiency and Renewable Energy
(EERE)
www.eere.energy.gov

Environmental Protection Agency
www.epa.gov

Geothermal Energy Association
www.geo-energy.org

DISCLAIMER

The websites listed on this page were active at the time of publication. The publisher is not responsible for websites that have changed their address or discontinued operation since the date of publication. The publisher will review and update the websites upon each reprint.

BIBLIOGRAPHY

Central Intelligence Agency, "The World Factbook — Country Comparison: Oil — Consumption," www.cia.gov/library/publications/the-world-factbook/rankorder/2174rank.html (April 30 2010).

Environmental Protection Agency, "Electricity Generation," www.epa.gov/energy/electricity.html (April 29 2010).

Environmental Protection Agency, "Climate Change," www.epa.gov/energy/climate.htm (April 29 2010).

Onetcenter.org, "Energy Brokers," online.onetcenter.org/link/summary/41-3099.01 (April 30 2010).

Onetcenter.org, "Energy Engineers," online.onetcenter.org/link/summary/17-2199.03 (April 30 2010).

Onetcenter.org, "Environmental Economists," online.onetcenter.org/link/summary/19-3011.01 (April 30 2010).

Onetcenter.org, "Fuel Cell Engineers," online.onetcenter.org/link/summary/17-2141.01 (April 30 2010).

Onetcenter.org, "Geothermal Production Managers," online.onetcenter.org/link/summary/11-3051.02 (April 30 2010).

Onetcenter.org, "Solar Energy Installation Managers," online.onetcenter.org/link/summary/47-1011.03 (April 30 2010).

Onetcenter.org, "Solar Energy Systems Engineers," online.onetcenter.org/link/summary/17-2199.11 (April 30 2010).

Onetcenter.org, "Sustainability Specialists," online.onetcenter.org/link/summary/13-1199.05 (April 30 2010).

Onetcenter.org, "Wind Energy Project Managers," online.onetcenter.org/link/summary/11-9199.10 (April 30 2010).

Onetcenter.org, "Wind Energy Engineers," online.onetcenter.org/link/summary/17-2199.10 (April 30 2010).

United States Department of Labor, Bureau of Labor Statistics, "Chemists and Materials Scientists," www.bls.gov/oco/ocos049.htm (April 30 2010).

United States Department of Labor, Bureau of Labor Statistics, "Engineers," www.bls.gov/oco/ocos027.htm (April 30 2010).

United States Department of Labor, Bureau of Labor Statistics, "Machinery Manufacturing," www.bls.gov/oco/cg/cgs052.htm (April 30 2010).

United States Department of Labor, Bureau of Labor Statistics, "On the Grids: Careers in Energy," www.bls.gov/ooq/2008/fall/art02.pdf (April 30 2010).

United States Department of Labor, Bureau of Labor Statistics, "Scientific Research and Development Services," www.bls.gov/oco/cg/cgs053.htm (April 30 2010).

United States Department of Labor, Bureau of Labor Statistics, "You're a What? Solar photovoltaic installer," www.bls.gov/opub/ooq/2009/fall/yawhat.pdf (April 30 2010).

INDEX

American Solar Energy Society 52, 54, 56
apprenticeship 43, 45

Bureau of Labor Statistics 37, 51–54

carbon cycle 21, 26
climate 8, 11–12, 53
coal 13–15, 17, 19, 21

dams 28-29, 38

economics 46, 52
electricity 14–17, 22–28, 56
emissions 9, 12–13, 16–19, 26, 28
energy broker 39–40
engineering 34–37
    education 44–45
environmental economist 40–41
Environmental Protection Agency (EPA) 12, 14, 23, 26, 54

fuel cell 33, 38

gasoline 9–10, 15, 33
greenhouse gases 11–17, 22, 35, 53

manufacturing
    education 45, 46
    jobs 37, 38

natural gas 17, 19, 21

Obama, Barack 55, 57

personality traits 18, 29, 41, 47, 57
photovoltaic (PV) 22–24, 39, 48, 56
Ph.D. 43–44

renewable energy
    biomass 25–26
    hydroelectricity 28–29
    landfill gas 26–27
    solar 22–24
    wind 27–28
research and development 32–33
    education 44

subsidies 51–52

turbine 27–28, 34–38

PICTURE CREDITS

Creative Commons Attribution
    Jen SFO-BCN: pg. 14

Fotolia.com
    Alphaspirit: pg. 50
    Alx: pg. 8
    Andrei Merkulov: pg. 30
    IRC: pg 11
    pf30: pg 20
    Rafa Irusta: pg. 42
    Tilio & Paolo: pg. 36

NASA: pg 16

National Science Foundation
    Zina Deretsky: pg. 25

United States Air Force
    Nadine Y. Barclay: pg. 23

United States Department of Energy: pg. 27, 33

About the Author

Camden Flath is a writer living and working in Binghamton, New York. He has a degree in English and has written several books for young people. He is interested in current political, social, and economic issues and applies those interests to his writing.

About the Consultant

Michael Puglisi is the director of the Department of Labor's Workforce New York One Stop Center in Binghamton, New York. He has also held several leadership positions in the International Association of Workforce Professionals (IAWP), a non-profit educational association exclusively dedicated to workforce professionals with a rich tradition and history of contributions to workforce excellence. IAWP members receive the tools and resources they need to effectively contribute to the workforce development system daily. By providing relevant education, timely and informative communication and valuable findings of pertinent research, IAWP equips its members with knowledge, information and practical tools for success. Through its network of local and regional chapters, IAWP is preparing its members for the challenges of tomorrow.